DAMAGE NOTED

Áll Holidays
—MENUS—

Barbara
Grunes

641.568

ideals

Ideals Publishing Corp.
Nashville, Tennessee

Contents

Director of Publishing Patricia Pingry
Managing Editor Marybeth Owens
Cookbook Editor Naomi Galbreath
Art Director William Scholz
Photographer Gerald Koser
Editorial Assistant Linda Robinson
Typography Kim Kaczanowski

A special thanks to Carole Janis for recipes and
food styling for the Gingerbread House.

ISBN 0-8249-3041-X
Copyright © MCMLXXXIV by Ideals Publishing Corp.
All rights reserved.
Printed and bound in the United States of America.

Published by Ideals Publishing Corporation
Nashville, Tennessee 37214
Published simultaneously in Canada

Cover Recipes
Aloha Dip, 4
Party Sandwich Loaf, 5
Apple Cider Punch, 45

Fisherman's Crab, 4

New Year's Eve Buffet

Menu for 10 to 12

Aloha Dip with Fresh Fruits • Eggnog
Spiced Mixed Nuts • Party Sandwich Loaf
Fisherman's Crab • Turkey French Toast
Teriyaki Kabobs • Hot Beef Sandwiches
Pasta Salad • Peach Oatmeal Bread
Apricot Squares • Chocolate Pound Cake

Aloha Dip

12 macaroons, crushed
¼ cup firmly packed light
  brown sugar
2 cups sour cream
  Pineapple chunks
  Assorted berries
  Peaches, sliced
  Melon chunks
  Kirsch *or* brandy, optional

In a bowl, stir together macaroons, sugar, and sour cream. Chill several hours to soften macaroon pieces. Do not stir again or macaroon pieces will break into small crumbs. Place chilled dip in center of a large platter. Arrange fruits of your choice in groups around dip. Sprinkle fruits with kirsch or brandy if desired.

Fisherman's Crab

½ cup margarine *or* vegetable oil
1½ cups sliced celery
1 pound mushrooms, sliced
½ cup chopped green onions
¼ cup chopped green pepper
4 cans (10¾ ounces *each*)
  cream of shrimp soup
1½ cups half-and-half
2 pounds crab meat, shell and
  cartilage removed
¼ cup diced pimiento
12 baked patty shells

In a large skillet or kettle, over low heat, melt margarine. Add celery; cook until celery is tender. Add mushrooms, green onions, and green pepper; cook until mushrooms are tender, stirring occasionally. Stir in soup, half-and-half, and crab meat. Heat until bubbly, stirring often. Fold in pimiento. Serve hot in patty shells.

Party Sandwich Loaf

1 unsliced sandwich loaf
(1½ pounds)
Ham Salad
Egg Salad
Cream Cheese Frosting
Assorted vegetables and
herbs for garnish

Remove crusts from sandwich loaf; slice into 7 layers lengthwise. Cover 3 layers with Ham Salad. Cover 3 layers with Egg Salad. Assemble loaf with alternate layers of ham and egg fillings. Wrap in plastic wrap; chill thoroughly. About 1 hour before serving, frost with Cream Cheese Frosting. Garnish as desired. Refrigerate until serving time.

Ham Salad

2 cups diced cooked ham
¼ cup chopped sweet pickle
2 tablespoons chopped onion
¼ cup mayonnaise, or as needed
to bind
¼ teaspoon prepared mustard

In a small bowl, combine all ingredients.

Egg Salad

4 hard-cooked eggs, chopped
1 stalk celery, chopped
1 teaspoon grated onion
1 teaspoon prepared mustard
3 tablespoons mayonnaise
Salt and pepper to taste
2 tablespoons chopped fresh
parsley

In a small bowl, combine all ingredients.

Cream Cheese Frosting

11 ounces cream cheese,
softened
2 tablespoons sour cream
2 teaspoons grated onion

In a small mixing bowl, beat together cream cheese, sour cream, and onion until smooth.

Note: Freeze juice or carbonated beverages in your ice cube tray for interesting additions to cold drinks. Or, add chunks of fruit or fresh mint leaves to water in ice cube trays before freezing.

New Year's Eve Buffet

Spiced Mixed Nuts

1 egg white
1 teaspoon cold water
1 pound mixed shelled walnuts,
    almonds, and pecans
½ cup sugar
½ teaspoon cinnamon
¼ teaspoon salt

Preheat oven to 225° F. Butter a cookie sheet. In a mixing bowl, beat egg white with cold water until bubbly. Add nuts; mix lightly until evenly coated. In a separate bowl, stir together sugar, cinnamon, and salt. Add nuts; toss until nuts are coated with sugar mixture. Arrange nuts evenly over prepared cookie sheet. Bake for 1 hour, stirring every 15 minutes.

Turkey French Toast

1 cup cooked minced turkey
1 tablespoon sweet pickle
    relish
¼ cup chopped celery
¼ cup mayonnaise
12 slices bread
3 eggs, lightly beaten
¾ cup milk
1 teaspoon sugar
4 to 6 tablespoons butter

In a mixing bowl, combine turkey, relish, celery, and mayonnaise. Spread on 6 slices of bread; top with remaining bread. In a shallow bowl, beat together eggs, milk, and sugar. In a large skillet, melt butter over medium heat. Dip both sides of one sandwich in egg mixture. Fry on both sides until golden brown. Repeat with remaining sandwiches. Cut on the diagonal into 24 triangles.

Pasta Salad with Pecans

1 pound spinach fettuccine,
    cooked according to package
    directions
¼ cup olive oil
3 cloves garlic, minced
1¼ cups chopped pecans
1 tablespoon basil
¼ cup chopped fresh parsley
½ teaspoon salt
½ teaspoon pepper
¼ cup freshly grated Parmesan
    cheese

In a serving bowl, toss pasta with olive oil. In a small bowl, combine garlic, pecans, and seasonings; mix well. Add pecan mixture to pasta; toss to coat. Stir in Parmesan cheese. Adjust seasoning. Chill until ready to serve.

Spiced Mixed Nuts

New Year's Eve Buffet

Teriyaki Kabobs

¼ cup soy sauce
½ teaspoon chopped candied ginger
½ teaspoon sugar
1 small clove garlic, pressed
1 pound sirloin steak, 1 inch thick, cubed
1 pineapple, cut into 1-inch cubes
24 small stuffed green olives

In a bowl, stir together soy sauce, ginger, sugar, and garlic. Add steak cubes; stir to coat with marinade. Marinate, covered, overnight in refrigerator. The next day, drain steak. Skewer steak cubes and pineapple chunks on small picks. Broil 3 inches from heat for 5 minutes; turn. Broil 3 minutes longer. Add an olive to each pick; serve hot.

Hot Beef Sandwiches

½ cup butter, divided
5 pounds sirloin top roast
¾ cup sherry
1 large Bermuda onion, sliced
2 tablespoons Worcestershire sauce
3 tablespoons freshly squeezed lemon juice
½ teaspoon salt
1 pound mushrooms, sliced
3 beef bouillon cubes, dissolved in 1½ cups hot water
Crusty rolls

Preheat oven to 325° F. In a large skillet, melt ¼ cup butter. Brown roast on all sides. Place roast on a rack in a large shallow roasting pan. Roast for 2 hours. Pour sherry over roast and roast 1 hour longer. Remove from pan; set aside to cool. Reserve pan juices. In a large skillet, heat remaining ¼ cup butter. Sauté onion until tender. Stir in Worcestershire sauce, lemon juice, salt, mushrooms, bouillon, and juices from roast. Simmer 5 minutes. Slice roast very thin. Place slices in roasting pan. Pour bouillon-mushroom mixture over meat. Bake, covered, for 45 minutes. Serve on crusty rolls.

Peach Oatmeal Bread

2 cups whole wheat flour
1 cup quick-cooking rolled oats
¾ cup sugar
3 teaspoons baking powder
½ teaspoon salt
½ teaspoon baking soda
½ teaspoon cinnamon
2 cups chopped peaches
2 eggs, well beaten
1 cup milk
¼ cup vegetable oil

Preheat oven to 350° F. Butter a 9 x 5-inch loaf pan. In a mixing bowl, stir together flour, oats, sugar, baking powder, salt, soda, and cinnamon. Add peaches; stir to coat with dry ingredients. In a separate bowl, beat eggs with milk and oil. Add to flour mixture, stirring just until dry ingredients are moistened. Pour into prepared pan. Bake for 1 hour. Cool in pan for 10 minutes; transfer to a wire rack to cool completely. Wrap in aluminum foil.

Apricot Squares

1 cup butter, room temperature
½ cup sugar
½ teaspoon vanilla
2 cups all-purpose flour
1 jar (12 ounces) apricot jam
2 egg whites
½ teaspoon almond extract
1 cup confectioners' sugar
½ cup slivered almonds

Preheat oven to 350° F. In a mixing bowl, cream butter, sugar, and vanilla until fluffy. Stir in flour; blend well. Spread mixture into a 9 x 13-inch pan. Bake for 15 minutes. Cool. Spread the jam over the crust. Beat egg whites with almond extract until soft peaks form. Gradually beat confectioners' sugar into egg whites until stiff peaks form. Spread egg white mixture over the jam. Sprinkle with almonds. Bake for an additional 15 to 20 minutes. Cool. Slice into bars.

Chocolate Pound Cake

6 tablespoons butter, room temperature
1¼ cups sugar
3 eggs
1¾ cups all-purpose flour
½ cup cocoa
1½ teaspoons baking powder
½ teaspoon baking soda
¼ teaspoon salt
¾ cup sour cream
1 teaspoon vanilla
1 teaspoon chocolate extract
Confectioners' sugar

Preheat oven to 325° F. Grease a 9 x 5-inch loaf pan. In a mixing bowl, cream butter and sugar until fluffy. Beat in eggs. In a separate bowl, stir together dry ingredients. Add sour cream alternately with dry ingredients to creamed mixture; blend well. Blend in vanilla and chocolate extract. Pour batter into prepared pan. Bake for 1 hour and 15 minutes or until cake tests done. Cool cake in pan. When completely cool, turn out of pan and sprinkle with confectioners' sugar.

Eggnog

8 eggs
¾ cup sugar
½ teaspoon salt
½ cup rum
1 teaspoon vanilla
1 quart milk
2 cups heavy cream
Nutmeg

In large bowl of electric mixer, beat eggs at high speed until thick and foamy. At medium speed, gradually add sugar and salt. Add rum and vanilla. At low speed, gradually add milk. Chill. Before serving, whip cream; fold into egg mixture. Pour eggnog into punch bowl. Garnish with ground nutmeg.

Chinese New Year Dinner

Menu for 8

Wintermelon and Ham Soup • Pork with Vegetables
Spicy Chicken • Sautéed Fish with Hoisin Sauce
Lion's Head • Roast Pork
Almond Cookies • Fortune Cookies

Pork with Vegetables

4 tablespoons black bean sauce
2 tablespoons soy sauce
2 tablespoons dry sherry
4 tablespoons peanut oil
2 slices ginger root (¼-inch-thick *each*), peeled and minced
4 cloves garlic, minced
2 carrots, diagonally sliced
2 green peppers, cut in strips
1 pound lean pork, sliced into thin 1½-inch-long strips
1 cup sliced water chestnuts
1 cup chicken stock
4 teaspoons cornstarch mixed with 4 teaspoons cold water
Sliced almonds, optional

In a small bowl, mix bean sauce, soy, and sherry. In a wok or large skillet over high heat, heat oil. Add ginger and garlic; stir-fry 30 seconds. Add carrot and green pepper; stir-fry 1 minute. Add pork and bean sauce mixture; stir-fry 3 minutes. Add water chestnuts and stock; cover; cook 1 minute or until carrots are tender-crisp. Uncover. Stir cornstarch mixture until smooth; add to wok. Simmer, stirring constantly, until sauce thickens. Serve immediately. Garnish with almonds.

Sautéed Fish with Hoisin Sauce

6 tablespoons peanut oil
1¼ pounds flounder fillets
2 cloves garlic, minced
2 slices ginger root, peeled and minced
2 tablespoons light soy sauce
2 tablespoons Hoisin sauce
2 tablespoons white wine
Salt and pepper to taste

In a heavy skillet, heat 3 tablespoons of the oil. Sauté fillets 5 minutes on each side or until fish flakes easily when tested with a fork. Drain on paper toweling. Arrange fish on a serving plate. In the skillet, heat remaining oil. Add garlic and ginger; stir-fry for 10 seconds. Add remaining ingredients; heat 10 seconds. Drizzle sauce over fish. Serve with hot fluffy rice.

Wintermelon and Ham Soup

1 pound wintermelon, peeled,
  halved, seeds and pith
  removed
10 cups chicken stock
1 slice boiled ham, cut into
  julienne strips
  Salt and pepper to taste

Cut the wintermelon into 1 x 2-inch-long strips. In a saucepan, heat chicken stock. Add melon, ham, salt, and pepper. Simmer for 30 minutes or until the melon is tender.

Spicy Chicken on Shredded Lettuce

10 leaves Boston lettuce,
  shredded
1 teaspoon cornstarch
1 tablespoon water
2 teaspoons cornstarch
1 egg white
1 teaspoon white wine
½ teaspoon sugar
2 whole chicken breasts, boned
  and cut into ½-inch strips
4 tablespoons peanut oil
½ teaspoon hot pepper flakes
1 teaspoon minced ginger root
½ teaspoon salt

Arrange lettuce on serving platter. In a small bowl, mix cornstarch and water; set aside. In a separate bowl, stir together cornstarch, egg white, wine, and sugar. Add chicken; stir to coat. In a wok or heavy skillet, heat oil to very hot. Add hot pepper flakes and ginger; stir-fry 10 seconds. Add chicken pieces and salt; stir-fry until chicken turns white and is cooked through, about 3 minutes. Stir cornstarch mixture; add to wok. Heat and stir until mixture thickens slightly. Arrange chicken over lettuce.

Lion's Head

1 pound ground pork
4 Chinese mushrooms, soaked
  and shredded
¼ cup water chestnuts, minced
2 green onions, chopped
2 cloves garlic, minced
1 egg, lightly beaten
½ teaspoon salt
½ teaspoon pepper
2 teaspoons cornstarch
4 tablespoons peanut oil
½ head Chinese cabbage, thinly
  sliced
1 cup chicken stock
2 tablespoons light soy sauce
1 tablespoon cornstarch

In a medium bowl, stir together first nine ingredients. Form into 1-inch balls. In a wok or heavy skillet, heat oil. Brown pork balls in oil; set aside. In the same skillet, stir-fry cabbage 1 minute. Add stock and soy sauce. Arrange pork balls over cabbage in skillet. Reduce heat. Simmer, covered, over medium-low heat for 45 minutes. Arrange cabbage and pork balls on a serving dish. Whisk cornstarch into liquid in pan. Simmer, stirring constantly, until sauce thickens. Drizzle sauce over pork balls.

Roast Pork

2 cloves garlic, minced
3 slices ginger, minced and peeled
4 green onions, chopped
4 tablespoons sherry
2 tablespoons light soy sauce
3 tablespoons Hoisin sauce (available at oriental food stores)
3 tablespoons chili sauce
½ teaspoon salt
½ teaspoon pepper
1 pork tenderloin (2½ to 3 pounds)
½ cup honey

Preheat oven to 325° F. In a large, shallow dish, combine garlic, ginger, onions, sherry, soy sauce, Hoisin sauce, chili sauce, salt, and pepper; blend well. Place pork tenderloin in marinade; turn to coat. Marinate 1 hour, turning once. Place tenderloin on a rack in a roasting pan. Roast for 1 hour, basting occasionally with honey. When pork is cool, cut thin slices. Serve with oriental noodles.

Almond Cookies

½ cup ground almonds
½ cup lard, room temperature
½ cup butter, room temperature
1 cup sugar
½ teaspoon salt
1 teaspoon almond extract
3 eggs
2¾ cups all-purpose flour

Preheat oven to 350° F. In a large mixing bowl, blend almonds, lard, butter, and sugar until fluffy. Mix in salt, almond extract, and eggs. Add flour; blend well. Cover batter; refrigerate 1 hour. Form into 1-inch balls. Place cookies on an ungreased baking sheet. Bake for 20 minutes. Transfer to a wire rack to cool. Makes 3 dozen cookies.

Fortune Cookies

2 egg whites
¼ cup sugar
½ teaspoon vanilla
5 tablespoons peanut oil
3 tablespoons cold water
1 cup flour
30 fortunes written on 3 x ¾-inch strips of paper

Preheat oven to 350° F. In a mixing bowl, stir together all ingredients, except fortunes, until blended. Drop batter by teaspoonfuls onto an ungreased cookie sheet, allowing 3 cookies per sheet. Bake for 5 minutes. Place fortunes in the center of each cookie. Fold cookie in half; pinch seam together. Fold corners down. Place each cookie in a cupcake tin to harden. Makes 30 cookies.

Oriental food stores are a pleasure to visit. Take advantage of their many kinds of soy sauce, noodles, dried mushrooms, and other seasonings, condiments, and snacks.

Valentine's Day Dinner

Menu for 2 to 4
Tuna Nuggets • Caponata
Tabouleh Stuffed Pork Chops
Herbed Cucumbers • Parsnips with Bacon
Chocolate Truffles • Strawberry Soufflé

Caponata

⅓ cup olive oil *or* vegetable oil
1 medium eggplant (about 1 pound), unpeeled, cubed
1 cup sliced onion
3 stalks celery cut into ½-inch pieces
1 can (15 ounces) tomato sauce with tomato bits
½ cup pitted ripe olives, halved
2 tablespoons capers
⅓ cup red wine vinegar
1½ tablespoons sugar
1 teaspoon salt
½ teaspoon pepper
Dark rye bread

In a large skillet over high heat, heat oil. Add eggplant, onion and celery. Sauté, stirring constantly for 10 minutes. Reduce heat to medium-low. Stir in remaining ingredients, except bread. Simmer, uncovered, stirring occasionally, until the mixture is thick and celery is still crisp. Spoon caponata into a bowl; cover. Chill at least 2 hours. Stir before serving. Serve with dark rye bread.

Tuna Nuggets

1 can (6½ ounces) tuna, drained and flaked
3 ounces cream cheese, room temperature
½ teaspoon lemon juice
1 teaspoon horseradish
Dash hot sauce
½ cup chopped fresh parsley

In a mixing bowl, stir together all ingredients, except parsley, until well mixed. Shape mixture into ½-inch balls. Roll tuna balls in parsley. Chill until serving time.

Strawberry Soufflé, 17

Tabouleh Stuffed Pork Chops _____

4 pork rib chops, cut 1¼ to 1½
   inches thick, trimmed of fat
¾ cup water
½ teaspoon salt
⅓ cup bulgur
½ cup shredded carrot
¼ cup chopped fresh parsley
2 green onions, chopped
1 teaspoon chopped fresh mint
   or ¼ teaspoon dried mint
1 tablespoon butter, melted
1½ teaspoons freshly squeezed
   lemon juice
¼ teaspoon salt
⅛ teaspoon ground allspice
   Freshly ground pepper
   to taste
2 tablespoons vegetable oil

With a sharp knife, cut an opening in the rib side of each chop, forming a pocket. Be careful not to cut through to the other side of chop. In a small saucepan, combine water and salt; bring to a boil. Stir in bulgur. Reduce heat, cover, and simmer over medium heat for 15 minutes. Add carrot; continue cooking, covered, for 10 minutes or until carrots are tender and water is absorbed. Remove from heat. Stir in parsley, green onions, mint, butter, lemon juice, and seasonings. Spoon about ½ cup stuffing mixture into each chop. In a large skillet, heat oil; brown chops on each side. Arrange chops in baking dish, cover and bake at 350° F. for 1 hour.

Parsnips with Bacon _____

4 slices bacon
1 pound parsnips, peeled and
   cut into julienne strips
1 small onion, minced
   Salt and pepper to taste
2 tablespoons chopped fresh
   parsley

In a large skillet, cook bacon until crisp. Transfer to paper towels to drain. Crumble bacon; set aside. To drippings in skillet, add parsnips and onion; toss to coat. Sprinkle with salt and pepper. Cook over low heat, covered, for 10 minutes or until vegetables are tender, stirring often. Add bacon and parsley to skillet. Stir well; serve.

Herbed Cucumbers _____

2 tablespoons salad oil
½ teaspoon salt
2 cucumbers, thinly sliced
1 large onion, sliced
2 tablespoons water
   Dash tabasco sauce
1 tablespoon crushed thyme

Heat oil with salt in a large skillet. Add cucumbers and onion. Cook over medium heat, stirring constantly, about 3 minutes. Add water, tabasco sauce, and thyme. Cover and cook, shaking skillet occasionally, for about 2 minutes or until onions are barely tender.

Chocolate Truffles

1 package (12 ounces) semisweet
  chocolate chips
¾ cup sweetened condensed
  milk
1 teaspoon vanilla
1½ cups vanilla wafer crumbs
2 tablespoons creme de café
  coffee liqueur
  Powdered cocoa

In top of double boiler over hot (not boiling) water, melt chocolate chips. Stir in condensed milk, vanilla, vanilla wafer crumbs, and liqueur. Beat until smooth. Refrigerate mixture about 45 minutes or until cool and easy to shape. With buttered hands, shape mixture into ¾-inch balls. Roll balls in cocoa.

Strawberry Soufflé

  Butter
  Granulated sugar
1 envelope unflavored gelatin
1 cup granulated sugar, divided
¾ cup cold water
3 cups fresh strawberries,
  hulled
4 eggs, separated
¼ teaspoon cream of tartar
  Red food coloring, optional
1 cup whipping cream, whipped

Butter bottom and sides of 1½-quart soufflé dish; sprinkle with sugar. Wrap a 4-inch band of aluminum foil, triple thickness, around the dish, overlapping 2 inches. Lightly butter inside of band and sprinkle with sugar. Fasten to soufflé dish so that collar extends 2 inches above rim of dish. In a medium saucepan, stir together gelatin and ¾ cup of the sugar. Stir in water; let stand 1 minute. Cook, stirring constantly, over low heat until gelatin dissolves completely, 5 to 8 minutes. Remove from heat. Mash strawberries; stir into gelatin. In a small bowl, beat egg yolks at high speed until thickened, about 5 minutes. Blend a little of the strawberry mixture into yolks. Add yolk mixture to strawberries; blend well. Chill, stirring occasionally, until mixture mounds slightly when dropped from a spoon, 30 to 45 minutes. Wash and dry beaters.

In a large bowl at high speed, beat egg whites and cream of tartar until foamy. Add remaining ¼ cup sugar, 1 tablespoon at a time, beating constantly until sugar is dissolved and whites stand in soft peaks. Beat in a few drops food coloring. Fold chilled gelatin mixture and whipped cream gently into egg whites. Pour into prepared dish. Chill until firm. Just before serving, carefully remove foil.

Easter Brunch

Menu for 6 to 8

Chili Dip for Shrimp
Potato Ham Boats
Eggs Benedict
Berry Mold
Orange Glazed Carrot Sticks
Banana Mocha Cake

Chili Dip for Shrimp

½ cup mayonnaise
½ cup sour cream *or* yogurt
2 tablespoons chopped sweet pickle
1 tablespoon chopped stuffed olives
2 teaspoons chili powder
1½ teaspoons grated or minced onion
1 hard-cooked egg, chopped

In a small bowl, combine all ingredients; mix well. Chill for several hours. Serve with shrimp.

Potato Ham Boats

8 large Russet potatoes
½ cup milk
4 tablespoons butter
2 eggs, well beaten
½ teaspoon salt
¼ teaspoon pepper
3 cups diced cooked ham
1 cup shredded sharp cheddar cheese, divided
½ cup minced green onion

Preheat oven to 400° F. Scrub potatoes; prick skins and bake for 50 to 60 minutes or until tender. Reduce oven temperature to 375° F. Cut potatoes in half lengthwise; scoop out pulp leaving a ¼-inch-thick shell. Mash pulp with milk, butter, egg, salt, and pepper. Stir in ham, ¾ cup cheese, and green onion. Spoon mixture into potato shells; bake at 375° F. for 20 minutes or until filling is lightly browned. Top with remaining cheese; return to oven and heat 5 minutes longer or until cheese melts.

Chili Dip for Shrimp
Peach Oatmeal Bread, 8

A GARDEN CLUB SUPPER
AT JOHN & LUCY'S

JULY 15
7:30 O'CLOCK

REGRETS ONLY
RSVP

Eggs Benedict

6 slices Canadian bacon (about 6 ounces)
1 tablespoon vegetable oil
3 English muffins, split and toasted
1 tablespoon vinegar
6 eggs
Blender Hollandaise Sauce
Paprika
Fresh watercress for garnish

In a heavy skillet, heat oil. Add Canadian bacon; sauté about 2 minutes on each side or until heated through. Place bacon on top of muffin halves; cover and keep warm. Add water to skillet to a depth of 1 inch. Stir in vinegar. Bring mixture to a boil; reduce heat. Break 1 egg into a shallow bowl; slip into water in skillet. Repeat with remaining eggs. Simmer, covered, for 3 to 5 minutes or until eggs are soft-cooked. Remove eggs with a slotted spoon and place over bacon; cover and keep warm. Prepare Blender Hollandaise Sauce. Spoon sauce over eggs. Sprinkle with paprika; garnish with watercress.

Blender Hollandaise Sauce

6 egg yolks
2 tablespoons freshly squeezed lemon juice
¼ teaspoon cayenne
1 cup butter

In a blender, place egg yolks, lemon juice, and cayenne. Process until smooth. In a small saucepan, heat butter until melted but not brown. With the blender running, pour butter into egg mixture in a slow, steady stream. Process a few seconds to thicken sauce.

Berry Mold

1 can (13½ ounces) crushed pineapple in syrup, drained, juice reserved
1 can (16 ounces) blueberries in water, drained, juice reserved
2 cups water
1 package (12 ounces) red raspberry-flavored gelatin
1½ cups sour cream
1 pint strawberries

In a saucepan, place reserved juice and 2 cups water. Bring mixture to a boil over medium heat. Remove from heat; stir in gelatin until dissolved. Set aside to cool. In a separate bowl, stir together pineapple, blueberries, and sour cream until sour cream is blended. Add fruit mixture to cooled gelatin; stir thoroughly. Pour into a lightly greased ring mold or heart mold. Chill until set, about 4 hours. Unmold; garnish with fresh strawberries.

Orange Glazed Carrot Sticks

1 pound carrots, pared and cut
  into julienne strips
3 tablespoons butter
¼ cup chopped onion
⅓ cup firmly packed light
  brown sugar
½ cup freshly squeezed orange
  juice
½ teaspoon salt

In a large skillet, cook the carrots, covered, in a small amount of water until tender. Remove carrots from skillet. In the same skillet, heat butter; add onion and cook until tender. Stir in brown sugar and orange juice; simmer 5 minutes. Add cooked carrots; sprinkle with salt. Simmer, spooning sauce over carrots until they are glazed and heated through.

Banana Mocha Cake

1 teaspoon instant coffee
  granules
1 cup mashed bananas (2 large
  bananas)
1¼ cups all-purpose flour
⅔ cup sugar
¼ cup cornstarch
3 tablespoons cocoa
1 teaspoon baking soda
½ teaspoon salt
1 egg, lightly beaten
⅓ cup vegetable oil
1 tablespoon vinegar
1 teaspoon vanilla
  Silky Mocha Frosting

Preheat oven to 350° F. In a small bowl, stir coffee into mashed bananas; blend well. In a 9-inch square baking pan, combine flour, sugar, cornstarch, cocoa, soda, and salt. Stir thoroughly with a fork. Make a well in the center of the dry ingredients. Place banana mixture, egg, oil, vinegar, and vanilla in the well. With a fork, stir dry ingredients into moist ingredients until well blended. Bake for 30 minutes. Cool completely before frosting with Silky Mocha Frosting.

Silky Mocha Frosting

3 tablespoons butter, softened
1½ cups confectioners' sugar
2 tablespoons cocoa
1 teaspoon instant coffee
  granules
2 tablespoons milk
½ teaspoon vanilla

In a small bowl, combine butter, sugar, cocoa, and coffee until well blended. Stir in milk and vanilla; beat until smooth.

Mother's Day Breakfast

Menu for 6

Blueberry Fruit Salad
Mom's Banana Breakfast Drink
Kids' Scrambled Eggs • Potato Waffles
Rhubarb Custard Kuchen • Brown Sugar Drops

Blueberry Fruit Salad

1 cup fresh blueberries
1 small banana, sliced
1 cup sliced strawberries
1 cup halved seedless grapes
2 cups cubed cantaloupe
4 tablespoons orange juice, divided
¼ cup mayonnaise
¼ cup plain yogurt
1 tablespoon honey
¼ teaspoon ground ginger

In a bowl, combine first 5 ingredients and 2 tablespoons of the orange juice; toss gently. In a separate bowl, stir together remaining orange juice, mayonnaise, yogurt, honey, and ginger. Chill. Arrange fruit on serving plates. Serve with honey yogurt dressing.

Kids' Scrambled Eggs

6 eggs
⅓ cup shredded Cheddar cheese
⅓ cup commercial sour cream
Salt and pepper to taste
8 slices bacon, cooked, crumbled
2 tablespoons butter

Beat eggs with fork until well beaten. Blend in cheese, sour cream, seasonings, and bacon; set aside. In a large skillet over medium heat, heat butter. Pour in egg mixture. As it cooks, stir gently with a spoon. Continue until the eggs are set.

Mom's Banana Breakfast Drink

1 egg
1 cup milk
1 small ripe banana
1 tablespoon honey
1 scoop vanilla ice cream

In a blender, combine egg, milk, banana, and honey; process until smooth. Pour into a tall glass; top with ice cream.

Mother's Day Breakfast

Potato Waffles

2 cups all-purpose flour
⅔ cup potato flakes
4 teaspoons sugar
4 teaspoons baking powder
1 teaspoon salt
4 eggs
3 cups skim milk
2 tablespoons vegetable oil

In a large bowl, mix flour, potato flakes, sugar, baking powder, and salt. In a small bowl, beat together eggs, milk, and oil. Add to dry ingredients; mix well. Bake batter on waffle iron according to manufacturer's directions until waffles are golden brown.

Rhubarb Custard Kuchen

1¼ cups all-purpose flour
½ teaspoon salt
1 teaspoon sugar
1 teaspoon baking powder
½ cup butter, room temperature
1 egg yolk
2 tablespoons milk
4 heaping cups rhubarb, diced
1⅛ cups sugar
2 egg yolks
1 tablespoon all-purpose flour
3 egg whites, beaten stiff
½ cup sour cream
1 tablespoon grated orange peel
¼ teaspoon salt

Preheat oven to 350° F. In a mixing bowl, stir together flour, salt, sugar, and baking powder. Blend in butter, egg yolk, and milk. Pat dough into a 9 x 13-inch baking pan. In a bowl, mix together rhubarb and sugar; spread over crust. In a separate bowl, beat egg yolks with 1 tablespoon flour until well blended. Fold in stiffly beaten egg whites. Fold in sour cream, orange peel, and salt. Pour custard over rhubarb. Bake for 45 minutes.

Brown Sugar Drops

¼ cup packed light brown sugar
¼ cup butter
¼ cup dark corn syrup
½ cup all-purpose flour
1 teaspoon ground ginger
⅛ teaspoon salt

Preheat oven to 375° F. In a large saucepan, place brown sugar, butter, and corn syrup. Cook and stir mixture over low heat until butter melts; remove from heat. Stir in flour, ginger, and salt until ingredients are well blended. Drop batter by rounded teaspoonfuls about 4 inches apart onto a greased and floured cookie sheet. Bake for 5 minutes or until cookies are set. Cool 2 minutes; remove with a spatula. Makes 2 dozen.

Memorial Day Family Gathering

Menu for 12

Salmon Mousse with Avocado Sauce
Artichoke Dip • Potato Skins
Cheesy Chicken • Two Lettuce Salad
Strawberry Malakoff • Black Bottom Cupcakes

Salmon Mousse with Avocado Sauce

2 tablespoons unflavored gelatin
¼ cup cold water
½ cup boiling water
1 can (16 ounces) salmon, boned
3 tablespoons lime juice
3 shallots, minced
1 cup heavy cream, whipped
½ cup boiling water
½ cup mayonnaise
1 teaspoon basil
  Avocado Sauce

In a small bowl, sprinkle gelatin over cold water; stir. Add ½ cup boiling water, stirring until gelatin is dissolved. In a large mixing bowl, combine remaining ingredients. Stir in gelatin. Mound salmon mixture in a lightly greased 4-cup fish or ring mold. Cover loosely; chill until set. Loosen sides of mold with spatula. Unmold onto serving platter; garnish with cucumber slices, parsley, and tomatoes. Serve with Avocado Sauce.

Avocado Sauce

½ cup sour cream
½ cup mayonnaise
3 tablespoons chopped fresh parsley
1 tablespoon lemon juice
1 teaspoon prepared mustard
2 avocados

In a blender or food processor, blend all ingredients.

Cheesy Chicken

2 chickens, cut into serving
   pieces
¾ cup margarine
2 cups flour
1½ cups grated Romano *or*
   Parmesan cheese
1 teaspoon salt
1 teaspoon pepper
1 teaspoon basil *or* **garlic**
   powder
1½ teaspoons paprika
2 tablespoons onion flakes
4 eggs
13 ounces evaporated milk

Preheat oven to 350° F. In a small pan, melt margarine; set aside. In a shallow pan, mix flour, cheese, salt, pepper, basil, paprika, and onion flakes. In a separate bowl, beat eggs and milk until blended. Dip each chicken piece in egg-milk mixture; roll in flour and cheese mixture. Place on a baking sheet. Sprinkle chicken with remaining cheese mixture; drizzle with melted margarine. Bake 60 to 75 minutes.

Two Lettuce Salad

3 tablespoons tarragon vinegar
½ teaspoon salt
¼ teaspoon pepper
¼ teaspoon vegetable oil
1 head Boston lettuce, trimmed,
   rinsed, and dried
4 heads Bibb lettuce, trimmed,
   rinsed, and dried
1 Belgian endive, trimmed,
   rinsed, and dried
¼ pound snow peas, trimmed
¼ pound bean sprouts, blanched
   Salt and pepper to taste
½ teaspoon tarragon

In a jar with a tight-fitting lid, combine vinegar, salt, pepper, and oil; shake to blend. Tear salad greens into bite-sized pieces directly into a salad bowl. Add snow peas and bean sprouts; toss to mix. Season with salt, pepper, and tarragon. Just before serving, shake the dressing to blend; pour over salad. Toss salad to coat with dressing.

Potato Skins

8 large baking potatoes,
   scrubbed, pricked
6 tablespoons unsalted butter,
   melted
2 cups shredded Cheddar
   cheese
½ pound bacon, cooked and
   crumbled

Bake potatoes at 400° F. for 1 hour or until tender. Cool. Reduce oven temperature to 375° F. Cut potatoes in half lengthwise; scoop out insides, leaving a ¼-inch-thick shell. Brush the insides of the potato skins generously with melted butter. Sprinkle the insides with cheese and bacon. Arrange skins on a cookie sheet. Bake for 30 minutes. Cut into strips.

Memorial Day Family Gathering

Artichoke Dip

1 can (14 ounces) artichoke
   hearts, drained and chopped
1 package (8 ounces) mozzarella
   cheese, shredded
1 cup grated Parmesan cheese
1 cup mayonnaise
1 teaspoon garlic powder
   Chopped fresh parsley

Preheat oven to 350° F. In a mixing bowl, stir together artichoke hearts, mozzarella, Parmesan, mayonnaise, and garlic powder until well mixed. Mound mixture in a 1-quart casserole. Bake for 25 minutes or until mixture is bubbly and top is light brown. Top with parsley. Serve with crusty bread.

Strawberry Malakoff

6 ounces ladyfingers
1 cup plus 2 tablespoons butter,
   room temperature
½ cup sugar
1¼ cups ground almonds
1 cup heavy cream
1¼ pints fresh strawberries,
   sliced; divided

Butter a 5-cup charlotte mold or a bowl with a 5-cup capacity. Cut waxed paper to fit the mold bottom; butter the paper. Line bottom and sides of mold with ladyfingers, cutting the ladyfingers to give a tight fit. In a mixing bowl, cream butter and sugar until fluffy. Stir in almonds. Whip heavy cream until soft peaks form; stir cream into almond mixture. Fold in 1 pint strawberries. Mound mixture in prepared mold. Cover with plastic wrap and refrigerate overnight or until set. When ready to serve, run a knife around side of the mold; invert onto serving dish. Carefully remove mold and paper. Garnish with remaining strawberries. Serve immediately after unmolding.

Black Bottom Cupcakes

2 large ripe bananas
1½ cups all-purpose flour
1 cup sugar
¼ cup cocoa
1 teaspoon baking soda
½ teaspoon salt
⅓ cup vegetable oil
1 teaspoon vanilla
1 large firm banana
6 ounces cream cheese, room
   temperature
⅓ cup sugar
1 egg
6 ounces semisweet chocolate
   chips

Preheat oven to 350° F. Slice ripe bananas into blender. Blend until pureed. In a mixing bowl, stir together flour, 1 cup sugar, cocoa, soda, and salt. Stir in the pureed bananas, oil, and vanilla. Spoon equal amounts of the mixture into 18 paper-lined muffin cups. Slice 2 slices of firm banana into each cup. In a mixing bowl, beat cream cheese with ⅓ cup sugar until fluffy. Blend in egg. Stir in chocolate chips. Spoon equal amounts of chocolate chip mixture into the muffin cups. Bake for 30 minutes. Cool in the pan on racks.

Father's Day Dinner

Menu for 10

Citrus Punch
Seven Layer Salad
Shish Kabobs
Carrots with Mint
Chocolate Nut Drop Cookies

Citrus Punch

1 can (46 ounces) chilled
   pineapple juice
1 can (46 ounces) chilled orange
   or grapefruit juice
2 quarts chilled ginger ale
1 pint lemon or lime sherbet

In a punch bowl, stir together juices and ginger ale. Scoop sherbet into punch bowl. Serve immediately.

Seven Layer Salad

1 head lettuce, sliced
2 green peppers, chopped
4 stalks celery, chopped
¼ pound fresh mushrooms,
   sliced
1 sweet onion, chopped
2 cups frozen peas, thawed
2 cups mayonnaise
2 teaspoons sugar
1 teaspoon salt
½ teaspoon garlic powder
½ teaspoon marjoram
1 cup grated Cheddar cheese
4 strips bacon, cooked crisp,
   crumbled

In a glass serving bowl with straight sides, layer lettuce, green pepper, celery, mushrooms, onion, and peas. In a mixing bowl, combine mayonnaise, sugar, salt, garlic powder, and marjoram; blend well. Spread mayonnaise mixture evenly over the peas. Sprinkle with Cheddar cheese and bacon. Cover and refrigerate for at least 4 hours or overnight. When serving, be sure each portion contains some of each salad layer.

Shish Kabobs

1 cup vegetable oil
1 cup red wine
3 bay leaves, crumbled
2 tablespoons wine vinegar
3 cloves garlic, crushed
½ teaspoon pepper
6 pounds chuck steak, cut into
   1½-inch cubes
1 pound large fresh mushrooms
9 medium white onions, peeled
   and quartered
6 large green peppers, cut into
   sixths
1 pint cherry tomatoes

In a bowl, stir together first 6 ingredients to make marinade. Place steak cubes in a large, shallow pan. Pour marinade over steak; stir to coat. Cover and refrigerate for 8 hours; stir occasionally. Oil 12 long skewers. Skewer meat alternately with vegetables, beginning and ending with meat. Broil or grill for a total of 15 to 20 minutes, turning once. Brush with marinade while cooking.

Carrots with Mint

2 pounds carrots, pared,
   trimmed, and thinly sliced
¾ cup heavy cream
   Salt and pepper to taste
2 tablespoons chopped fresh
   mint leaves

In a large saucepan, bring 2 cups water to a boil. Add carrots. Simmer until tender, about 10 minutes; drain. Stir in cream, salt, and pepper; heat through. Sprinkle carrots with fresh chopped mint leaves.

Chocolate Nut Drop Cookies

¼ cup butter, room temperature
¼ cup peanut butter
½ cup sugar
1 extra large egg
¼ cup milk
½ teaspoon vanilla
½ cup all-purpose flour
¼ teaspoon baking powder
¼ teaspoon baking soda
½ teaspoon salt
½ cup rolled oats
3 ounces semisweet chocolate
   chips
⅓ cup chopped nuts

Preheat oven to 375° F. In a mixing bowl, blend butter and peanut butter. Add sugar, egg, milk, and vanilla; blend well. In a separate mixing bowl, stir together flour, baking powder, soda, salt, and oats. Blend dry ingredients into peanut butter mixture. Stir in chocolate chips and nuts. Drop by teaspoonfuls onto an ungreased baking sheet. Bake for 10 to 12 minutes or until cookies are golden brown. Makes about 35 cookies.

Fourth of July Celebration

Menu for 10 to 12
Stuffed Edam Cheese • Garden Potato Salad
Salmon Steaks in Aspic • Charcoal Broiled Sirloin Steak
Deep Dish Apple Pie • Yankee Doodle Dandy Pie

Stuffed Edam Cheese

1 Edam cheese (1 pound)
4 tablespoons beer
1 tablespoon butter
½ teaspoon Worcestershire sauce
¼ teaspoon Tabasco sauce
¼ cup chopped pecans

With a knife or cookie cutter, cut a round of wax from top of cheese. Scoop out cheese, leaving a ½-inch-thick shell. In a mixing bowl, stir together cheese and remaining ingredients until creamy and well blended. Mound back into the cheese shell. Refrigerate for 1 hour before serving. Serve with crackers and crisp sliced vegetables.

Garden Potato Salad

5 hard boiled eggs, chopped
2½ pounds small potatoes, cooked, peeled, and sliced
1 medium onion, chopped
1 cucumber, peeled and chopped
1 cup chopped celery
1 cup chopped tomatoes
½ cup sliced radishes
1 teaspoon salt
½ teaspoon pepper
Seasoned salts to taste
1½ cups mayonnaise
½ cup milk
Paprika

Set aside ¼ cup of the chopped egg for garnish. In a mixing bowl, stir together remaining eggs, potatoes, vegetables, and seasonings. In a small bowl, blend mayonnaise and milk. Pour mayonnaise mixture over vegetables; mix well. Garnish with reserved egg and paprika.

Salmon Steaks in Aspic

6 salmon steaks, 1 inch thick
6 peppercorns, crushed
1 teaspoon salt
4 sprigs fresh dill
1 small onion, sliced
1 stalk celery, chopped
1 carrot, sliced
4 cups boiling water
2 envelopes unflavored gelatin
½ cup freshly squeezed lemon
 juice
 Cucumber slices, lemon slices,
 and olives

Place fish in a large skillet. Add seasonings, vegetables, and boiling water. Cover and simmer for about 8 minutes or until fish flakes easily. Do not overcook. Cool fish in cooking liquid; transfer to a platter. Carefully remove skin and bones. Strain cooking liquid; return liquid to skillet. Soften gelatin in lemon juice; add to liquid in skillet. Heat, stirring constantly, until gelatin dissolves. Pour gelatin mixture into a bowl; refrigerate until just beginning to thicken.

Pour half of the gelatin mixture into a 13 x 9-inch baking dish. Arrange salmon steaks in the dish. Spoon remaining gelatin mixture over fish. Chill until firm. Cut around each salmon steak, leaving a border of gelatin. Arrange salmon on a lettuce-lined platter. Garnish with cucumber slices, lemon slices, and olives.

Charcoal Broiled Sirloin Steak

1 sirloin steak (5 pounds), 1½ to
 2 inches thick, trimmed of fat
⅓ cup vegetable oil
⅓ cup red wine vinegar
2 cloves garlic, crushed
1 teaspoon basil
½ teaspoon salt
½ teaspoon pepper

Slash fatty edge of steak at 1-inch intervals. Place steak in a large pan. In a bowl, stir together remaining ingredients; pour over steak. Chill, covered, 2 to 3 hours, turning several times. Start charcoal fire 30 to 40 minutes before cooking time. Coals are ready when glowing and covered with gray ash. Rub hot grill with a bit of fat trimmed from steak. Grill 5 to 6 inches above coals on both sides, brushing occasionally with marinade. Allow about 25 minutes for rare, 30 minutes for medium on an open grill. To test for doneness, make a small slash in center of steak.

Fourth of July Celebration

Yankee Doodle Dandy Pie

1 package (3½ ounces) vanilla
  pudding mix
8 ounces cream cheese,
  softened
½ teaspoon vanilla
1 graham cracker piecrust
  (8 inches)
20 to 25 strawberries, hulled
1 pint blueberries
  Whipped cream or topping,
  optional

Prepare pudding mix according to package directions; remove from heat. Beat in cream cheese and vanilla until mixture is smooth. Pour filling into crust. Refrigerate 3 hours or overnight. Arrange strawberries in circle around outer edge of pie. Place 1 large strawberry in center of pie. Fill in remaining area with blueberries. Serve with whipped cream, if desired.

Deep Dish Apple Pie

1½ cups all-purpose flour
½ teaspoon salt
3 tablespoons butter, room
  temperature
2 tablespoons vegetable
  shortening, room temperature
1 egg yolk
4 to 6 tablespoons ice water

In a large mixing bowl, stir together flour and salt. Cut in butter and shortening until the mixture resembles coarse crumbs. Add egg and water; mix until mixture holds together. Gather dough into a ball; knead lightly. Cover with plastic wrap. Chill for 1 hour.

8 large firm cooking apples
½ cup granulated sugar
½ cup firmly packed light brown
  sugar
2 teaspoons grated lemon peel
1 teaspoon cinnamon
3 tablespoons butter, cut into
  ½-inch pieces

Preheat oven to 425° F. Butter a deep-dish 9-inch pie plate. Peel, core and slice apples. Place apples in a large mixing bowl. Toss with granulated sugar, brown sugar, and lemon peel. Place in buttered pie pan. Sprinkle with cinnamon; dot with butter.

3 tablespoons milk
3 tablespoons sugar
  Cheddar cheese

On a lightly floured board, roll crust to a 10-inch round. Fit crust over filling. Seal crust and flute edges. Make a ½ inch vent in center of crust. Brush crust with milk; sprinkle with sugar. Bake 15 minutes. Reduce heat to 350° F. Bake for 35 minutes or until crust is golden brown. Serve with Cheddar cheese.

Labor Day Dinner for the Family

Menu for 8

Anchovy Appetizer
Apple Date Salad
Stuffed Breast of Veal
Noodle Ring
Chocolate Acorns
Cream Puffs

Apple Date Salad

½ cup plain yogurt
3 tablespoons freshly squeezed lemon juice
1 tablespoon honey
24 whole pitted dates
3 stalks celery, sliced
2 firm, tart apples, cored and sliced
½ cup walnuts, halved
Butter lettuce leaves

In a small bowl, stir together yogurt, lemon juice, and honey; chill. Quarter the dates and add to the dressing together with celery, apples, and walnuts. Spoon mixture onto a bed of lettuce and serve.

Anchovy Appetizer

1 can (2 ounces) anchovy fillets
1 clove garlic, minced
2 tablespoons olive oil
1 tablespoon red wine vinegar
1 tablespoon tomato paste
1 tablespoon finely minced ripe black olives
1 tablespoon grated onion
6 slices firm white bread

In a bowl, crush anchovies with a fork. Stir in all other ingredients, except bread, and mash to make a paste. Under the broiler, toast bread on one side only. Spread the untoasted side with the anchovy mixture, pressing down firmly. Place under the broiler; broil until light brown. Cut into quarters.

Stuffed Breast of Veal

1 breast of veal (about 5 pounds)
  boned, with pocket
  Salt and pepper to taste
4 tablespoons butter, divided
1 onion, minced
½ pound fresh mushrooms,
  sliced
¼ pound ground veal
1½ cups breadcrumbs
2 tablespoons fresh minced
  parsley
2 eggs, lightly beaten
¼ cup heavy cream
¼ teaspoon nutmeg
  Flour
1 medium onion, sliced
2 carrots, sliced
¼ teaspoon thyme
¼ teaspoon rosemary
2 bay leaves
1 cup chicken stock
1 cup dry wine

Season veal with salt and pepper. In a large skillet, heat 2 tablespoons of the butter. Add onion; sauté until tender. Add mushrooms; sauté until tender, stirring occasionally. Stir in ground veal; sauté 3 minutes, stirring often. Remove from heat; stir in breadcrumbs, parsley, eggs, cream, and nutmeg. Stuff breast with the mixture; close the opening with skewers or string.

Preheat oven to 350° F. Heat remaining butter in a roasting pan. Dredge veal lightly in flour. Brown in hot butter on all sides; remove from pan. In the roasting pan, place onion and carrots. Return meat to pan with remaining ingredients. Roast, covered, for about 1½ hours. Turn meat once or twice. Remove cover; add more broth if needed. Roast, basting often with pan juices, for another hour or until meat is tender and browned.

Note: In recipes calling for chicken stock, you may use homemade or canned broth, or use bouillon made with instant granules and boiling water.

Noodle Ring

¼ cup butter
½ cup firmly packed dark brown
  sugar
½ cup pecan halves
½ pound thin egg noodles,
  cooked according to package
  directions
2 eggs, lightly beaten
¼ cup butter, melted
1 teaspoon cinnamon
1 teaspoon nutmeg
½ cup sugar
½ teaspoon salt

Preheat oven to 350° F. In the bottom of a 6-cup mold, melt butter. Add brown sugar; press mixture into bottom of pan. Press pecans firmly into butter, flat side up, in an attractive pattern. Place noodles in a large mixing bowl. Add remaining ingredients; toss to mix. Place noodles over topping in mold. Bake for 1 hour. Unmold onto a serving platter.

Labor Day Dinner for the Family

Chocolate Acorns

3 egg whites
1 tablespoon vinegar
¼ teaspoon salt
1 cup sugar
1 teaspoon vanilla
½ pound blanched ground
    almonds
4 squares, 1 ounce each,
    unsweetened chocolate
1 cup semisweet chocolate
    chips, melted
½ cup finely chopped pistachios

Preheat oven to 250° F. In a large mixing bowl, beat egg whites until soft peaks form. Beat in vinegar and salt. Add sugar; continue beating until stiff peaks form. Fold in vanilla, almonds, and unsweetened chocolate. Drop by heaping teaspoonfuls 1 inch apart onto a greased cookie sheet. Bake for 25 to 30 minutes. When cookies are cool, dip halfway into melted chocolate, then roll in pistachios. Makes 5 dozen.

Cream Puffs

½ cup butter *or* margarine
1 cup water
1 cup all-purpose flour
¼ teaspoon salt
4 eggs
    Confectioners' sugar
    Chocolate syrup, if desired

Preheat oven to 400° F. In a saucepan, melt butter. Add water; bring to a boil. In a bowl, stir together flour and salt. Add to water all at once; stir vigorously. Cook, stirring constantly, until mixture forms a ball and leaves side of pan. Remove from heat; cool 5 minutes. Add eggs, 1 at a time, beating well after each addition. Drop batter by heaping tablespoonfuls 3 inches apart onto cookie sheets. Bake 30 minutes until golden brown and puffed. Remove from oven; split. Remove any uncooked dough. Fill with ice cream or whipped cream. Dust with confectioners' sugar. Drizzle with chocolate syrup.

Halloween Party for the Kids

Menu for 6 to 8

Witches' Brew Cider
Hot Dog Surprises
Skillet Sombrero Pie
Monster Cookies
Caramel Apples

Witches' Brew Cider

4 cups apple cider
2 cans (6 ounces *each*) frozen
  lemonade concentrate,
  thawed
2 cups water
8 cinnamon sticks
  Lemon slices

Into a large saucepan, pour cider, lemonade concentrate, and water; stir. Over medium heat, bring cider to a simmer. Pour into cups. Place a cinnamon stick and a lemon slice in each cup.

Hot Dog Surprises

8 hot dogs, minced
⅓ cup grated American cheese
2 hard-boiled eggs, peeled and
  chopped
3 tablespoons pickle relish
1 teaspoon prepared mustard
½ teaspoon garlic salt
8 hot dog buns

Preheat oven to 375° F. In a large mixing bowl, stir together all ingredients except buns. Partially hollow out centers of buns; fill with hot dog mixture. Wrap each bun in aluminum foil, sealing securely. Place on cookie sheets. Bake for 10 to 12 minutes.

Skillet Sombrero Pie

1 pound ground beef
1 package (10 ounces) frozen
  corn, thawed
1 can (8 ounces) tomato sauce
1 can (16 ounces) tomatoes
1 tablespoon instant minced
  onion
1 package (1¾ ounces) chili
  seasoning mix
1 package (6 ounces) corn chips
½ cup grated Cheddar cheese

In a large skillet over medium heat, sauté beef until browned. Stir in corn, tomato sauce, tomatoes, onion, and seasoning mix. Reduce heat. Simmer 10 minutes. Arrange chips in ring around edge of skillet. Sprinkle cheese over meat mixture; heat until cheese melts, 3 to 5 minutes. Serve pie directly from skillet.

Caramel Apples

1½ cups chopped peanuts
6 firm apples, washed and dried
1 teaspoon vanilla
1 teaspoon baking soda
¾ cup sugar
½ cup butter
⅛ cup white corn syrup

Place peanuts in a shallow bowl; set aside. Insert wooden skewers into the stem end of apples. In a small dish, stir together vanilla and baking soda; set aside. In a heavy saucepan, place sugar, butter, and corn syrup. Cook over medium heat, stirring to blend. Continue to cook until mixture reaches 300° F. on a candy thermometer. Stir in vanilla mixture. Dip and twist apples in hot caramel until coated. Roll apples in nuts. Place on waxed paper to harden.

Monster Cookies

2 eggs
½ cup butter *or* margarine,
  softened
½ cup packed light brown sugar
½ cup granulated sugar
½ cup peanut butter
1 teaspoon vanilla
1½ cups flour
½ cup quick-cooking rolled oats
1 teaspoon baking soda
1 package (7 ounces) candy-
  coated chocolate pieces *or*
  1 package (6 ounces)
  semisweet chocolate chips

Preheat oven to 350° F. In a mixing bowl, stir together eggs, butter, brown sugar, granulated sugar, peanut butter, and vanilla; blend well. Stir in remaining ingredients. For each cookie, drop 2 tablespoons dough 3 inches apart on baking sheet. Bake 10 to 12 minutes. Remove cookies from baking sheet to a wire rack to cool. Store in an airtight container.

Thanksgiving Brunch

Menu for 12

Clam Dip • Scallop Mousse
Baked Canadian Bacon • Cucumber and Onion Salad
Pumpkin Bread • Treasure Toffee Cake
Brie in a Coat • Apple Cider Punch

Clam Dip

16 ounces cream cheese
1 cup sour cream
2 cans (6½ ounces *each*) minced
  or chopped clams, drained
2 green onions, chopped
¼ cup finely chopped pimiento
2 teaspoons finely chopped
  jalapeno pepper
2 tablespoons lemon juice
2 teaspoons Worcestershire
  sauce

In a mixing bowl, beat cream cheese with sour cream until well blended. Stir in remaining ingredients. Cover and chill. Serve with corn or tortilla chips.

Scallop Mousse

5 tablespoons butter
4 tablespoons all-purpose flour
½ teaspoon salt
¼ teaspoon white pepper
¼ teaspoon nutmeg
1 cup heavy cream
2 cups milk
4 eggs
2 pounds scallops, pureed

Preheat oven to 350° F. Butter a 2-quart casserole. Place casserole in a slightly larger pan filled with water to a depth of 2 inches. In a large saucepan over medium heat, melt butter; whisk in flour until flour is absorbed. Add salt, pepper, and nutmeg. Blend in heavy cream and milk; heat and stir until mixture thickens. Remove from heat. Add eggs, 1 at a time, beating well after each addition. Stir in scallops. Pour into prepared casserole. Bake for 65 minutes.

Baked Canadian Bacon

3 pounds Canadian bacon
1 orange, cut into thin slices
   Whole cloves
½ cup molasses
¼ cup water
½ cup orange juice
¼ cup sugar
¼ teaspoon dry mustard

Preheat oven to 325° F. Remove casing from bacon and place, fat side up, in a baking pan. Bake for 2 hours. Attach orange slices to bacon with cloves. In a small bowl, mix together remaining ingredients. Pour over bacon. Bake, basting often, for 30 minutes.

Cucumber and Onion Salad

4 medium cucumbers, peeled and sliced thin
2 large Bermuda onions, sliced very thin
1 cup fresh chopped mint *or* parsley
½ cup red wine
1 cup salad oil
5 shallots *or* green onions, minced
   Salt and pepper to taste

Arrange cucumbers in an overlapping circular pattern on a large salad plate. Scatter onions over cucumbers. In a jar with a tight-fitting lid, combine vinegar, oil, shallots, salt, and pepper. Shake to blend. Drizzle salad dressing over vegetables. Sprinkle with chopped mint.

Pumpkin Bread

1 cup firmly packed light brown sugar
½ cup granulated sugar
1 cup cooked *or* canned pumpkin
½ cup vegetable oil
2 eggs, beaten
2 cups all-purpose flour
1 teaspoon baking soda
½ teaspoon salt
½ teaspoon nutmeg
½ teaspoon cinnamon
½ teaspoon ginger
1 cup golden raisins
½ cup chopped walnuts
¼ cup water

Preheat oven to 350° F. Oil a 9 x 5-inch loaf pan. In a mixing bowl, stir together brown sugar, granulated sugar, pumpkin, oil, and eggs. Beat until blended. In a separate bowl, stir together flour, soda, salt, and spices. Add to pumpkin mixture; blend well. Stir in raisins, nuts, and water. Spoon into prepared loaf pan. Bake for 65 to 75 minutes or until a wooden pick inserted near the center comes out clean. Cool in the pan for 10 minutes. Turn out on a wire rack to cool completely.

Apple Cider Punch

2 quarts apple cider
4 cups cranberry juice
2 cups orange juice
2 cans (12 ounces) apricot
nectar
2 cups sugar
4 sticks cinnamon
Orange slices studded with
whole cloves

In a large kettle, combine all ingredients except orange slices. Simmer for 15 to 20 minutes. Garnish punch with floating clove-studded orange slices. Serve hot.

Treasure Toffee Cake

¼ cup sugar
1 teaspoon cinnamon
¼ teaspoon nutmeg
2 cups flour
1 cup sugar
1½ teaspoons baking powder
1 teaspoon baking soda
¼ teaspoon salt
1 teaspoon vanilla
1 cup sour cream
½ cup butter, softened
2 eggs
¼ cup chopped nuts
3 chocolate toffee bars
(1⅛ ounces *each*), coarsely
crushed
¼ cup melted butter
Confectioners' sugar

Preheat oven to 325° F. Butter and flour a 10-inch bundt pan. In a small bowl, stir together cinnamon and sugar. In a mixing bowl, combine remaining ingredients except nuts, candy bars, and melted butter. Beat until all ingredients are well blended and the batter is light. Spoon half of the batter into prepared pan. Sprinkle with 2 tablespoons cinnamon-sugar mixture. Spoon remaining mixture into pan. Top with remaining cinnamon-sugar mixture. Top with nuts and chopped candy. Pour melted butter over all. Bake 45 to 50 minutes. Cool in pan 5 minutes. Remove from pan; dust with confectioners' sugar.

Brie in a Coat

12-inch round of Brie, paper
wrapping removed
½ cup confectioners' sugar
½ cup sliced almonds

Place brie on a cookie sheet. Sprinkle sugar evenly over the cheese. Arrange the sliced almonds in an attractive pattern over sugar. Preheat the broiler to 450° F. Place cheese under the broiler for 1½ minutes or just until the sugar melts and starts to bubble. Serve with sliced fresh fruit.

Thanksgiving Dinner

Menu for 10 to 12

Cranberry Pineapple Salad
Carrot Curls and Radish Fans
Zucchini Custard Casserole
Roast Turkey with Wild Rice Stuffing
Brussels Sprouts • Sweet Potato Bake
Braided Filled Onion Loaf
Pecan Pie
Lace Cookies
Cranberry Jelly Candy

Cranberry Pineapple Salad

1 can (8 ounces) crushed pineapple, packed in juice, drained; reserve juice
2 tablespoons lemon juice
1 package (3 ounces) raspberry-flavored gelatin
1 can (14 ounces) cranberry sauce
¾ cup chopped celery

In a saucepan, mix together reserved juice, ½ cup water, and lemon juice; bring to a boil. Remove from heat; add gelatin; stir until gelatin dissolves. Add cranberry sauce; stir thoroughly. Refrigerate until mixture begins to set. Stir in pineapple and celery. Refrigerate until firm.

Brussels Sprouts

2½-3 pounds small brussels sprouts, ends trimmed and cut with an "X"
¼ cup butter
1 tablespoon prepared mustard
Salt and pepper to taste

In a saucepan, cook brussels sprouts in boiling salted water until barely tender, about 10 minutes; drain. In a large skillet, heat butter. Stir in mustard and simmer until blended, stirring constantly. Add brussels sprouts; toss to coat. Season with salt and pepper.

Sweet Potato Bake

1 can (8 ounces) pineapple
    chunks packed in juice,
    undrained
5 cups mashed sweet potatoes
    or yams
½ teaspoon salt
2 tablespoons butter
1 small package miniature
    marshmallows
⅓ cup pecan halves

Preheat oven to 350° F. Cut pineapple chunks in half. In a bowl, stir together pineapple chunks and juice, potatoes, salt, and butter. Place half of the potato mixture in a buttered casserole. Top with half the marshmallows. Add remaining potato mixture. Arrange pecans on top. Cover and bake for 30 minutes. Remove cover for last 10 minutes of baking. Add remaining marshmallows. This can be made the night before and refrigerated. Add the nuts and remaining marshmallows just before baking.

Zucchini Custard Casserole

1 pound zucchini
1 teaspoon salt
¼ cup chopped onion
6 eggs
1 cup milk
½ teaspoon basil
½ teaspoon oregano
2 tablespoons all-purpose flour
2 cups shredded Cheddar
    cheese, divided

Preheat oven to 350° F. Cut zucchini crosswise into ¼-inch slices, then into quarter slices. Place zucchini in colander; set colander in a bowl or in the sink. Sprinkle zucchini with salt; stir thoroughly. Let stand for 10 minutes. In a medium saucepan, bring 1 cup water to a boil. Add zucchini and onion. Simmer, covered, over medium heat until zucchini is tender-crisp, about 5 to 7 minutes; drain. Turn into a 9 x 9-inch baking dish or shallow 1½-quart casserole. Beat eggs, milk, and seasonings with fork until blended. Sprinkle flour over zucchini and toss lightly. Pour in egg mixture, then add 1½ cups of the cheese. Bake about 30 minutes, or until knife inserted near center comes out clean. Sprinkle remaining cheese over top of casserole.

Carrot Curls and Radish Fans

1 pound carrots
2 packages radishes

With a vegetable parer, cut carrots into thin lengthwise strips. Roll up slices; secure with wooden picks. In a bowl filled with ice cubes and water, place carrot curls. Slice radishes with parallel cuts reaching almost to stem end; do not cut through. Place radishes in the ice water with carrot curls. When ready to serve, drain vegetables; remove picks.

Braided Filled Onion Loaf

1 package active dry yeast
¼ cup lukewarm water
4 cups all-purpose flour
¼ cup sugar
1½ teaspoons salt
½ cup hot water
½ cup milk
¼ cup butter, room temperature
1 egg
¼ cup butter, melted
¾ cup finely chopped onion
1 tablespoon freshly grated
   Parmesan cheese
1 tablespoon sesame seed
1 teaspoon garlic salt

In a large mixing bowl, dissolve yeast in water. Add 2 cups of the flour, sugar, salt, water, milk, ¼ cup butter, and egg. Stir until all ingredients are blended. Gradually stir in remaining flour until dough leaves sides of bowl. Place dough in an oiled bowl; turn to oil dough. Cover loosely and place in a warm area to rise until doubled in bulk, about 1¼ hours. Preheat oven to 350° F. In a bowl, mix together melted butter, onion, Parmesan cheese, sesame seed, and garlic salt. Punch down dough. On a lightly floured board, knead dough until smooth and elastic. Roll dough to a 12 x 18-inch rectangle. Spread filling on dough. Cut dough lengthwise into three 4 x 18-inch strips. Roll up each strip lengthwise; seal edges. On a buttered cookie sheet, braid strips, keeping seam sides down. Set bread aside to rise in a draft free area for 1 hour. Bake for 45 to 50 minutes. Cool on a wire rack.

Roast Turkey

1 turkey (10 to 12 pounds)
   Wild Rice Stuffing
1 cup melted butter *or*
   margarine

Preheat oven to 325° F. Stuff neck and body cavities of turkey with Wild Rice Stuffing. Truss bird and place on a rack in a shallow roasting pan. Roast, uncovered, 4 hours or to an internal temperature of 190° F. When turkey begins to brown, cover lightly with a tent of aluminum foil. Baste occasionally with butter during roasting.

Wild Rice Stuffing

3 cups chicken broth *or* bouillon
1 cup raw wild rice
½ cup butter
1 cup diced celery
1 can (4 ounces) mushrooms
¼ cup minced onion
   Salt and pepper to taste
½ teaspoon sage

In a saucepan, bring broth to a boil; add rice. Simmer, covered, 30 to 45 minutes or until broth is absorbed. In a skillet, melt butter; sauté celery, mushrooms, and onion for 3 minutes. Stir in seasonings. Stir vegetable mixture into cooked rice.

Pecan Pie

¼ cup butter, room temperature
½ cup sugar
1 cup light corn syrup
¼ teaspoon salt
3 eggs
1 cup pecan halves
1 9-inch unbaked pastry shell
Sweetened whipped cream

Preheat oven to 350° F. In a mixing bowl, cream butter with sugar until fluffy. Add corn syrup and salt; blend well. Add eggs, 1 at a time, beating well after each addition. Stir in pecans. Pour into pie shell and bake for 50 minutes or until a knife inserted in the center of the filling comes out clean. Cool and serve with whipped cream.

Cranberry Jelly Candy

1 can (16 ounces) jellied cranberry sauce
3 packages (3 ounces *each*) cherry, raspberry or orange-flavored gelatin
1 cup sugar
½ bottle (3 ounces) liquid fruit pectin
1 cup chopped nuts
Additional sugar *or* flaked coconut

Place cranberry sauce in a saucepan; beat until smooth. Bring to a boil over medium heat. Stir in gelatin and sugar; simmer 10 minutes, stirring frequently until gelatin is dissolved. Remove from heat. Stir in fruit pectin. Add nuts and stir 10 minutes to keep nuts from floating. Pour into buttered 9-inch square pan. Chill until firm, about 2 hours. Sprinkle sugar or flaked coconut on a sheet of waxed paper. Turn candy out onto paper; cut into ¾-inch squares with spatula dipped in warm water. Roll each square in sugar. After about an hour, roll in sugar again to prevent stickiness.

Lace Cookies

¼ cup butter
¼ cup vegetable shortening
½ cup light corn syrup
¾ cup packed light brown sugar
1 cup unsifted all-purpose flour
¾ cup ground pecans
1 cup semisweet chocolate pieces

Combine butter, vegetable shortening, corn syrup, and sugar in a medium saucepan; bring to a boil. Remove from heat. Mix in flour and nuts. Drop batter by rounded teaspoons onto a greased and floured cookie sheet, 3 inches apart. Bake at 325° F. for 8 to 10 minutes. Cool 1 minute, remove from cookie sheet with a spatula. Melt chocolate in the top of a double boiler over hot (not boiling) water, stirring until smooth. Brush each cookie with chocolate.

Christmas Open House

Menu for 10-12

Strawberry Punch
Spiced Wine
Seafood Crepes
Turkey Quiche
Lamb Ring with Potato Puffs
Holiday Slaw
Anchovies and Pimientos
Orange Madeleines
Chocolate Kirsch Cake
Gingerbread House

Strawberry Punch

½ gallon vanilla ice cream, softened
2 quarts strawberry soda
2 quarts ginger ale
1 quart strawberries, hulled

In a punch bowl, place ice cream, strawberry soda, and ginger ale. Stir to blend. Add strawberries. Let stand for 1½ hours. Stir before serving.

Spiced Wine

3 quarts claret
Grated peel of 3 oranges
Grated peel of 3 lemons
12 cinnamon sticks
1½ teaspoons nutmeg
12 whole cloves, tied in a cheesecloth bag
6 tablespoons sugar

In a large kettle, simmer all ingredients for 10 minutes. Remove cloves before serving.

Turkey Quiche

1 frozen deep dish pie shell
4 cups cubed cooked turkey
½ cup chopped onion
1 tomato, chopped
4 ounces Monterey Jack cheese
4 ounces Cheddar cheese
1 cup sour cream
1 teaspoon tarragon
¼ teaspoon garlic powder
5 eggs, lightly beaten

Preheat oven to 350° F. In frozen pie shell place turkey, onion, and tomato. In a small bowl, stir together Monterey Jack and Cheddar. Sprinkle ½ of the cheese mixture over ingredients in pie shell. Add sour cream and seasonings to eggs. Pour egg mixture into pie shell. Top with remaining cheese. Bake for 45 minutes or until set.

Lamb Ring with Potato Puffs

2 pounds lean ground lamb
3 eggs, divided
½ cup chopped green pepper
2 tablespoons minced onion
1 tablespoon fresh chopped parsley
1 teaspoon salt
¼ teaspoon pepper
3 cups mashed potatoes

Preheat oven to 350° F. In a large bowl, combine lamb, 2 eggs, green pepper, onion, parsley, salt, and pepper; blend well. Press mixture into an 8-inch ring mold. Bake at 350° F. for 1 hour. Spoon off any accumulated fat. Unmold onto a shallow non-stick baking pan. Beat remaining egg into mashed potatoes. Mound potatoes around lamb ring. Raise oven temperature to 425° F. Bake for 10 minutes or until potatoes are lightly browned.

Holiday Slaw

1 head cabbage, shredded
1 onion, minced
1 red bell pepper, chopped
1 green pepper, chopped
1 cup mayonnaise
4 tablespoons red wine vinegar
3 tablespoons sugar
Salt and pepper to taste

In a deep bowl, toss cabbage, onion, and peppers. In a bowl, stir together remaining ingredients. Stir mayonnaise mixture into vegetables. Cover and chill until ready to serve.

Anchovies and Pimientos

3 jars (6 ounces *each*) sweet roasted peppers, drained and cut into strips
3 cans (2 ounces *each*) anchovies
2 tablespoons olive oil
3 cloves garlic, minced
1 teaspoon oregano

Arrange peppers attractively on a serving platter. Drain anchovies; arrange over peppers. Sprinkle with olive oil, minced garlic, and oregano. Cover loosely and chill until ready to serve.

Christmas Open House

Seafood Crepes

8 tablespoons butter
6 tablespoons flour
2 cups half-and-half
1 cup milk
½ cup sherry
2 cups lightly packed shredded
   brick cheese, divided
1½ pounds small shrimp
12 ounces scallops, sliced
1 pound mushrooms, sliced
2 tablespoons chopped pimiento
2 tablespoons chopped green
   pepper
1 teaspoon Worcestershire
   sauce
2 teaspoons salt
   Dash Tabasco sauce
28 Crepes

Prepare Crepes; set aside. Preheat oven to 350° F. In a 2-quart saucepan over medium heat, melt 6 tablespoons butter. Stir in flour. Cook, stirring constantly, until smooth and bubbly. Add half-and-half and milk; bring to a boil, stirring constantly. Boil 1 minute. Add sherry and 1 cup cheese. Heat and stir over low heat until cheese melts. Set aside. In a large skillet, melt remaining butter; sauté shrimp, scallops, and mushrooms until mushrooms are tender. Remove from heat. Stir in remaining ingredients and 1½ cups cream sauce. Place about ¼ cup seafood mixture down center of each of 28 Crepes; fold sides over to enclose filling. Spread ½ cup cream sauce evenly over the bottom of two 9 x 13-inch baking pans. Place Crepes seam sides down in pans. Pour remaining sauce over center of Crepes. Bake, covered, 25 minutes. Uncover; sprinkle cheese evenly over center of each Crepe. Bake for 2 minutes or until cheese melts. Sprinkle with paprika.

Crepes

2 eggs
1 cup plus 2 tablespoons milk
1 cup flour
1 tablespoon vegetable oil
⅛ teaspoon salt
2 tablespoons melted butter

In a medium bowl, beat eggs. Add milk, flour, oil, and salt. Beat again until batter is smooth. Cover and refrigerate 2 hours. Preheat a 6 or 8-inch omelet pan. Brush with a little of the butter. Pour about 3 tablespoons batter into pan and cook 2 to 3 minutes, rotating pan as batter is poured. Cook until lightly browned on bottom. Loosen edges with spatula and gently lift crepe. Stack between pieces of waxed paper. Keep covered. Makes 14.

Orange Madeleines

3 eggs
1 tablespoon freshly squeezed orange juice
1 cup sugar
2 tablespoons grated orange peel
1⅓ cups cake flour
½ teaspoon baking powder
¼ teaspoon salt
½ cup butter, melted and cooled
Confectioners' sugar

Preheat oven to 350° F. Butter and flour madeleine pan (available in gourmet shops). Beat eggs, orange juice, and sugar in a large mixing bowl. Continue beating until light and fluffy. Mix in orange peel. Sift together flour, baking powder, and salt. Stir in butter. Fill molds half-full with batter. Bake 12 minutes. Unmold cookies onto a serving plate. Refill mold and repeat until all batter is used. Sprinkle madeleines with confectioners' sugar.

Chocolate Kirsch Cake

8 eggs, separated, room temperature
1 cup sugar
1 teaspoon vanilla
8 tablespoons kirsch, divided
3 ounces semisweet chocolate, melted
1 cup cake flour
1 semisweet chocolate bar (8 ounces)
3 cups heavy cream
½ cup confectioners' sugar
1 can (16 ounces) sour pitted cherries, drained
10 whole maraschino cherries with stems

Preheat oven to 350° F. Butter and flour two 8-inch layer cake pans. In a small mixing bowl, combine egg yolks, sugar, vanilla, and 4 tablespoons kirsch. Beat until mixture doubles in volume. Add chocolate in a slow steady stream, mixing until blended. Sprinkle flour over mixture; blend well. Beat egg whites into chocolate batter. Pour batter into prepared cake pans. Bake for 15 to 20 minutes, or until cake tests done. Invert cakes on a rack; cool. Over waxed paper, scrape chocolate bar with a vegetable peeler to make chocolate curls. Freeze chocolate curls until ready to use. Whip cream until it begins to thicken. Gradually sprinkle sugar, 4 tablespoons at a time, over cream, beating until all the sugar has been added and soft peaks form. Cut each cake layer into 2 layers with a serrated knife. Place 1 layer on a serving platter. Sprinkle 1 tablespoon of kirsch over cake. Spread layer with whipped cream. Arrange ⅓ of the sour cherries over cream. Repeat layers twice. Top with remaining cake layer. Spread remaining whipped cream around sides and top of cake. Gently arrange chocolate curls on sides of cake. Decorate top of the cake with stemmed cherries. Chill cake until ready to serve.

Gingerbread House

Gingerbread Dough

5 cups shortening
5 cups brown sugar, packed
5 tablespoons cinnamon
6 tablespoons ginger
10 eggs
5 cups dark corn syrup
8 teaspoons baking soda
28 cups flour

Cream shortening, sugar, and spices in a large mixing bowl. Beat in eggs. Add corn syrup; blend well. Mix baking soda and flour together in separate bowl. Add ½ of the flour mixture to creamed ingredients; beat well. Stir in remaining flour mixture; beat until smooth. Wrap airtight. Chill at least 5 hours or overnight. Makes enough dough for house, trees, reindeer, and fence in photo.

Decorator Icing

4 pounds confectioners' sugar
12 egg whites
2 teaspoons cream of tartar

In a large mixing bowl, beat all ingredients together for about 10 minutes or until stiff peaks form. Cover with damp towel; take out only as needed, as this frosting hardens quickly. Note: Icing may be stored for several days in refrigerator. Beat again before using.

Christmas Wreath Candy

⅓ cup butter or margarine
20 marshmallows
   Green food coloring
2¼ cups cornflakes

Prepare this candy just before you plan to use it, as it hardens quickly. In microwave or top of double boiler, melt butter and marshmallows. Add food coloring as desired. Remove from heat. Add cornflakes and stir until well coated.

For assembly and decorating instructions, see page 59.

To cut out house:

Draw pattern pieces on cardboard or paper according to sizes indicated below, or as desired. Cut out pattern. On lightly greased, *inverted* cookie sheet, roll out dough to $3/16''$ thickness. Dust pattern pieces with flour. Place patterns on dough. Cut through dough with sharp knife. Without moving cut-out pieces, remove patterns and excess dough. Bake in place on *inverted* cookie sheet at 375° F. until lightly browned. Check cookie edges once during baking, straightening edges with a knife, if necessary. When dough is baked and still warm, loosen pieces with spatula. Do not remove from cookie sheets until completely cool. Use same dough and same procedure to make trees, reindeer, and fence, rolling dough somewhat thinner for smaller pieces. Cut tree cookies using pattern pictured. Shape reindeer using cookie cutters. For fence, cut strips of dough in varying lengths. Let baked dough sit 5-6 hours before assembling house.

To assemble house:

Use pastry bag with number 4 or 5 tip throughout assembly process. Mortar house with decorator icing, beginning with sides, front and back of house. Wherever seams meet, mortar with icing and press together gently. Prop pieces up with cans until icing sets. Wait overnight before putting on roof. Then thickly mortar with icing where front and back and side pieces meet roof. Press pieces together carefully. Mortar along seam at peak of roof. Assemble chimney pieces and mortar to roof. Let set 1 to 2 hours before decorating.

To decorate house:

Using same decorator icing and pastry bag, ice 12 vanilla wafers and dust with red sprinkles. Secure wafers with decorator icing, as pictured. Loop shingles of icing on roof. Thickly squiggle icing unevenly on edges of roof to simulate snow. Ice life savers to side of house. Line silver beads along roof top.

Decorate front of house with jelly rings, life savers, gumdrops, and red hots as pictured. Outline door with icing; attach gumdrop door knob; set aside.

With Christmas Wreath Candy, form wreath around door. Accent with red candy or icing to resemble holly. Mortar or set door in place, leaving slightly ajar.

Outline path with decorator icing and peppermint candy. Mortar gingerbread fence pieces together; place where desired. Sprinkle trees and reindeer lightly with sifted confectioners' sugar. Sprinkle confectioners' sugar around house to simulate snow. Fluff cotton to simulate chimney smoke.

Pattern Specifications:

> walls (2 pieces): 4″ x 12″
> roof (2 pieces): 14″ x 11″
> front and back: 12″ x 12″, cutting to form
>   roof peak, window, and door

Christmas Dinner

Menu for 10

Hot Crabmeat Appetizer
Ham Balls
Citrus Salad
Sour Cream Scalloped Potatoes with Ham
Broccoli Casserole
Glazed Cornish Game Hens
Sicilian Cake

Hot Crabmeat Appetizer

2 tablespoons milk
16 ounces cream cheese, softened
2 cans (6½ ounces *each*) flaked crabmeat
¼ cup instant chopped onion
1 teaspoon cream-style horseradish
1 teaspoon salt
White pepper to taste

Preheat oven to 375° F. In a small bowl, combine milk and cream cheese; blend well. Blend in remaining ingredients. Mound in a baking dish. Bake for 15 minutes. Serve hot with crackers.

Ham Balls

1 pound ground beef
1 pound ground ham
2 eggs
1½ cups cracker crumbs
1 cup firmly packed light brown sugar
1 teaspoon prepared mustard
½ cup water
½ cup vinegar

Preheat oven to 350° F. In a large bowl, mix together beef, ham, eggs, and cracker crumbs until well blended. Shape into balls; place on a large, rimmed baking sheet. In a separate bowl, stir together remaining ingredients until well blended. Pour over ham balls. Bake 1½ hours. Makes about 60.

Citrus Salad

8 large oranges, peeled and
  thinly sliced
2 medium Bermuda onions,
  thinly sliced
¼ cup olive oil
¼ cup red wine vinegar
½ teaspoon salt
½ teaspoon white pepper
1 head Boston lettuce

In a mixing bowl, mix oranges and onions. In a jar with a tight-fitting lid, combine oil, vinegar, salt, and pepper. Shake until blended. Pour over oranges and onions; toss lightly to mix. Arrange lettuce on chilled salad plates. Arrange tossed oranges and onions on lettuce.

Sour Cream Scalloped Potatoes with Ham

2 slices (½-inch thick *each*)
  smoked ham
8 medium potatoes, sliced thick
1 can (10¾ ounces) condensed
  cream of mushroom soup
1 cup sour cream
1 teaspoon salt
1 cup sliced onions
½ teaspoon white pepper
1 cup shredded Cheddar cheese

Preheat oven to 325° F. Butter a 3-quart casserole. Cut ham into 8 serving pieces. Slice potatoes. Combine soup, sour cream, salt, and pepper. In prepared casserole, alternate layers of ham, potatoes, and onions with sour cream mixture, ending with sour cream. Top with shredded cheese. Cover casserole loosely with aluminum foil. Bake for 2½ hours.

Broccoli Casserole

2 packages (10 ounces *each*)
  frozen cut broccoli
2 eggs, well beaten
1 can condensed Cheddar
  cheese soup
½ teaspoon crushed oregano
1 can (8 ounces) stewed
  tomatoes, cut up
3 tablespoons freshly grated
  Parmesan cheese

Cook frozen broccoli in unsalted water 5 minutes or until broccoli is tender. Drain well. In a mixing bowl, combine beaten eggs, soup, and oregano; stir in stewed tomatoes and broccoli. Pour mixture into a 10 x 6-inch baking dish. Sprinkle with Parmesan cheese. Bake uncovered at 350° F. for 30 minutes or until heated through.

Glazed Cornish Game Hens

10 Cornish game hens
  Salt and pepper to taste
  Butter
  Garlic powder
  Paprika
½ teaspoon melted butter
1 jar (12 ounces) currant jelly

Preheat oven to 350° F. Sprinkle inside of hens with salt and pepper. Tie legs together with string. Rub hens with softened butter; season to taste with garlic powder and paprika.

Place hens on a rack in a shallow pan. Brush with melted butter. Roast for 1 hour, basting once with melted butter. In a saucepan, heat currant jelly. Spoon over hens. Return hens to oven; roast, basting occasionally, an additional 30 minutes or until hens are tender and browned. Transfer hens to a serving platter. Remove strings. Spoon remaining warm jelly over hens.

Sicilian Cake

1 baked pound cake
⅓ cup dark rum
1 pound creamed ricotta cheese
⅓ cup sugar
¾ cup semisweet chocolate bits, chopped
⅓ cup candied cherries
⅓ cup candied orange peel
2 tablespoons all-purpose flour
  Chocolate Frosting

Cut cake into 4 horizontal layers with a serrated knife. Sprinkle rum over cake layers; set aside. In a mixing bowl, beat cheese and sugar until fluffy. Stir in chocolate. In a small bowl, toss cherries and orange peel with flour. Place fruit on a breadboard or in a food processor; chop coarsely. Add chopped fruit to cheese mixture; stir thoroughly. Place one layer of cake on a serving platter. Spread with ⅓ cheese mixture. Repeat until all 4 cake layers are stacked. Do not cover top of cake with cheese mixture. Cover cake with plastic wrap; refrigerate for 1 hour. Frost top and sides of cake with Chocolate Frosting. To serve, cut into very thin slices.

Chocolate Frosting

3 cups confectioners' sugar
3 ounces unsweetened chocolate, melted and cooled
¼ cup butter
1 egg yolk

Sift sugar into a large mixing bowl. Stir in chocolate, butter, and egg yolk. Beat until smooth.

Index